Life as Woman

20 Rules & Principles for Living as Rasta Empress

BY

Empress Yuajah

JAH RASTAFARI PRAYERS

JAH RASTAFARI
PRAYERS

Empress Yuajah

RASTA WAY OF LIFE

RASTA WAY
OF LIFE

RASTAFARI
LIVITY BOOK
EMPRESS
YUAJAH

HOW TO BECOME A RASTA

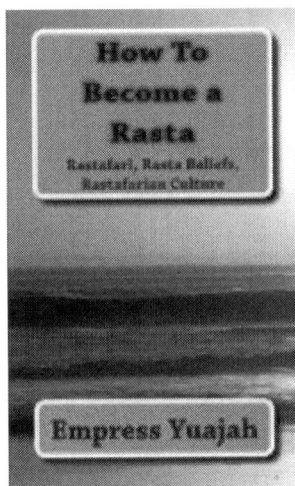

RASTAFARI: BELIEFS & PRINCIPLES

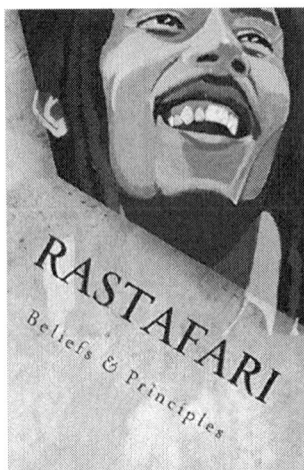

DEDICATION

To all women who know they were born a Queen.
Allow Jah to guide you to Embrace Divine Your Royal
Highness.

Contents

#1 Rastafari Empress Rules for Raising Children

Empress must raise their children with Respect and Righteousness. This means Rastafari women treat their children the way they themselves would like to be treated as children.

More importantly Empress Raise their children and show them Respect *as Creations of Jah*. We know and understand that children have "just arrived," and are still learning. We show children love understanding and patience. It is our duty as Rastafari to show our own children and the children of others, that Rastafari women are different.

Rastafari women are always aware that we are here to leave an impression in the minds of children so that they too will grow up and want to be Rastafari.

I always enjoy being around children. I try to make them feel as if I respect them and am interested in the things they are interested in. I show children great amounts of respect but most importantly I try to make sure they always see me happy and smiling so that they may know Jah resides in me, and that love is more important to me as an Empress than anything else. I leave that imprint, it is my duty.

This is the loving power of Jah.

If it is your goal as an Empress, to raise your children as Rastafari, all the same rules apply.

#2 Rastafari Empress Rules for Clothing and Attire

Rasta Empress is allowed to wear...

- Skirts below the Knee
- T-shirts
- Dress shirts
- Tights under a long shirt
- Tights with the buttocks area covered by a sash/scarf

Rasta Empress is not allowed to wear...

- Jeans pants
- Any pants (In Rastafari we believe pants are to be worn by men)
- Tight shirts accentuating the breast area
- Anything with skulls or Guns etc.
- Upside down crosses

Rasta Women are encouraged to wear

- Jamaican Flag colors/ emblem on Clothing
- Ethiopian Flag colors /emblem on Clothing
- Red Yellow and Green Earrings, Clothing and other accessories
- Natural fibres
- Marcus Garvey, King Selassie I T-shirts
- Long comfortable Skirts down to the ankles
- Dress shirts
- Robes also called a "Moo Moo"
- Army combat Gear (army print, army Jacket, army boots)
- Long comfortable dresses to the ankle
- Dreadlocks / Hair wrapped in a Turban

The long comfortable dress to the ankles is my favorite because it feels so feminine and I just know that it is pleasing to Jah for me to dress in this manner. I love to share my feminine beauty without looking or feeling trashy.

4 Reasons why Rasta Empress Dress the way they do?

1. **Respect our Royal Ancestry** - Accentuate and acknowledge our Royal Ancestry and Faith as the Feminine Divine Power. (Long Skirts and Dresses)

2. **Jah Power** - Represent a power that existed and still exists of our Lord and Savior King Selassie I who Defended Ethiopia in the 1935, when Italy Invaded Ethiopia. (Army Gear)

3. **Ancestral Roots and Culture** - Represent that we maintain our connection to our ancestors as we embrace our "Roots and Culture" Heritage. (Red Yellow and Green)

4. **Not of Babylon -** Separate ourselves as *Living in Babylon but not of it.* We are not brainwashed by media images of how women must be dressed because Rasta women are women of Jah, not of Babylon.

(Cover our breasts and buttocks, and wear loose clothes as opposed to tight clothing) It's a matter of feminine self-respect.

Yes, sometimes when I go out people stare, because of the way I dress. But I have come to realize the way I dress and how people react to me is more telling about them than it is about me. I keep in mind that I dress this way not to please Babylon, but for Jah.

#3 Rastafari Empress Rules concerning Friendship

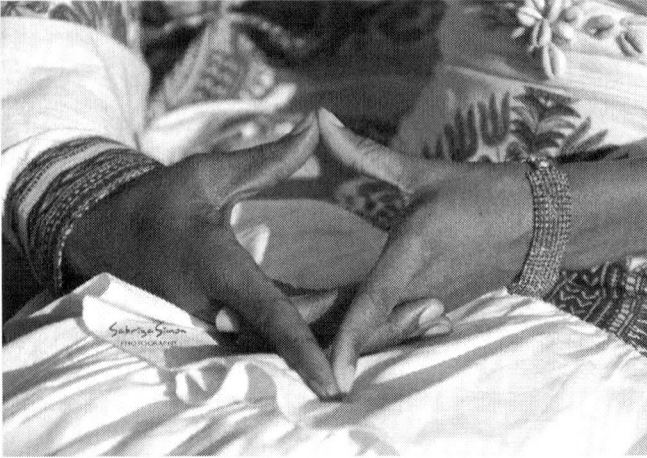

General Rules concerning friendship for Rastafari Women

Rastafari Women are not allowed to go to the homes of those who are not Rastafari. Those persons may enter *our* homes, in the hopes that they may encounter the power of King Selassie I, Jah Rastafari.

To learn more about How to handle
friendships as Rasta read my new book
entitled

"Rasta Bible: Rastafari Spiritual Wisdom"

Rastafari Women are discouraged from having the following friendships

- With those who work in the sex trade
- With those who do not believe in Jah (God)
- With those who live a lifestyle that breaks Jah 10 commandments (i.e. stealing, adultery, worshipping idols, giving false testimony against others etc.)

Rastafari Women are encouraged to have the following friendships

- Friendship with other Rastafari men and women
- Friendship with those who believe in Jah and keep his commandments
- Those who Respect the faith of Empress

- Those who maintain a positive philosophy of Love and brotherhood/sisterhood
- With those who enjoy learning about Rastafari and the Life of King Selassie I.

As Rasta we are very particular about the company we keep. We know over time we become just like those who we spend our time with. Rasta Empress keeps friends with those who think clean, treat others with kindness and respect, and those who choose to live in love at all times.

We do not hang out with those who use "dirty words" or who disrespect our spiritual beliefs or who use sex as a form of entertainment. We as Rasta do not keep friends with people who hurt others and want us to be a part of it.

I had to release a friendship because of this type of mentality in someone very close to me. I had to put my faith first

On Judgement day a me one a go stand up before Jah, so me cyan do tings fi cause Jah fi vex wid me just because of "friendship." No.

#4 Rasta woman Rules for Food and Eating

astafari women are encouraged to Say a prayer before eating which acknowledges that...

1. Jah has allowed her to have the food to eat today
2. To ask Jah to bless the food

Rastafari Prayer before Eating

"I an I give thanks, oh Jah for this meal you have blessed me with today. Please bless this food oh Jah, that it may nourish my body and give I an I strength. You are my provider oh Jah. Rastafari. "

A Rastafari women's Diet

Rasta women may eat a strictly Ital food diet. This means no meat, and no pork, chicken is optional. Many Rasta love to eat fish. But not all fish is for a Rastafari. Empress only eats fish *with scales*. Some Empress eats chicken. However I have been told if a Ras eats chicken, he or she will be "weak" as a Rasta. Based on my own spiritual observations and experiences. I would say yes it is best to avoid chicken all together.

Empress Diet while pregnant or nursing

Rastafari women are encouraged to eat more earth foods, fruits and vegetables for strength and vitality while pregnant or nursing. Empress are encouraged to eat more greens to build up the blood after giving birth. Empress are discouraged from eating packaged foods and foods with an overabundance of sugar or caffeine at this time as well..

Rasta people stay away from salt. Some use sea salt when cooking. Empress knows salt has caused many health problems in the black Caribbean community.

I use to cook with salt, but Jah has been showing me lately I really don't need to. The food has its own taste and it's ok to enjoy the food just the way it is. Jah doesn't like when Rasta use salt. He prefers us to enjoy the food the way he intended it to taste.

#5 Rasta woman Spiritual Obligations

Rasta Empress has many spiritual obligations, but they all boil down to one main goal. *To enter holy mount Zion and Rest in peace in the holy presence of Jah.*

Rasta Woman Spiritual Sabbath day Obligations

- To fast on the holy Sabbath and to clean the house

Rasta Woman spiritual obligations to her children

- To read the bible to her children or to ensure they read their bible 1 hour per day on their own.

Rasta Woman daily spiritual obligations

- To read her bible at least a minimum of 1 hour per day alone in silence. Bible readings may be done in 2 /30 minute sessions.
- To meditate in Silence to still her mind and allow Jah in. (15 minutes/day)
- To Know and to live by the *10 Rasta Rules for Living* (The 10 Commandments)

Rasta Women make time for Jah

- Jah time is very important. It's a time for Jah that strengthens the relationship an Empress has with him.
- During Jah time an Empress is to sit in silence for at least 15 - 30 minutes only getting up to pee but not to eat. (eating changes the focus of the spirit)
- Sit in silence and contemplate the day. But no talking.

Make time for Jah, and he makes time for Empress. Jah time should take place any time Empress is alone in the home. And should take place at least 3 times per week.

I like to spend some of my Jah time reading my bible too.

10 Life Rules for Empress

The Ten Commandments of the Christian Bible are the "life rules" for all Rasta.

1. "You shall have no other gods before[a] me.
2. "You shall not make for yourself an image in the form of anything in heaven above or on the earth beneath or in the waters below. 5 You shall not bow down to them or worship them; for I, the Lord your God, am a jealous God, punishing the children for the sin of the parents to the third and fourth generation of those who hate me, 6 but showing love to a thousand generations of those who love me and keep my commandments.
3. "You shall not misuse the name of the Lord your God, for the Lord will

not hold anyone guiltless who misuses his name.

4. "Remember the Sabbath day by keeping it holy. [9] Six days you shall labour and do all your work, [10] but the seventh day is a Sabbath to the Lord your God. On it you shall not do any work, neither you, nor your son or daughter, nor your male or female servant, nor your animals, nor any foreigner residing in your towns. [11] For in six days the Lord made the heavens and the earth, the sea, and all that is in them, but he rested on the seventh day. Therefore the Lord blessed the Sabbath day and made it holy.

5. "Honor your father and your mother, so that you may live long in the land the Lord your God is giving you.

6. "You shall not murder.

7. "You shall not commit adultery.

8. "You shall not steal.
9. "You shall not give false testimony against your neighbor.
10. "You shall not covet your neighbours' house. You shall not covet your neighbour's wife, or his male or female servant, his ox or donkey, or anything that belongs to your neighbour."

#6 Rasta Woman Hygiene and grooming

Perfume and body Odours

A bad body odour is not a part of the Rastafari Livity, However, Rasta women *do not* use perfume. We know Perfume is made up of ...

- Skunk spray
- Gasoline
- Bleach

And other chemicals that gives of a strong odour, and may be harmful to our bodies and the environment.

Rastafari women do our Research for health

We Rasta women research everything before we keep it in our home, or put it on our bodies, or ingest it as food.

Rasta women wear *natural essential oils* for a nice scent when going out, but rely heavily on bathing and natural deodorant.

We Rasta women also try to avoid behaviors common to prostitution work. Perfumes are made to simulate...stimulate what? We (Empress) do not participate.

Natural Deodorant

Rasta women wear natural deodorant because it is healthier to do so. The main ingredient in *non-natural* deodorant that you might purchase at your average drug store is <u>Aluminum.</u> Aluminum is not healthy for any woman to put under her arm pits directly beside her breasts.

#7 Rasta woman Rules concerning Makeup

I know many Rasta women are told they must not wear makeup. Yes, it is "higher" spiritually speaking not to embrace Babylon lies....however....as a woman of Jah, I know it is not sinful to wear makeup.

Rasta women may wear makeup as long as the colors are natural, and some other things are kept in mind. It is worse to

LIFE AS A RASTA WOMAN

drink alcohol than to wear a little makeup as a Rastafari Empress.

- Rasta women do not wear false eyelashes
- Rasta women do not wear makeup that is purple or blue, or pink or white or black in color

35

Rasta women are encouraged to wear makeup that is

- Flesh tones
- Natural looking
- Naturally made (without animal products) Rastafari are pro life
- Light weight
- Green yellow and red are allowed in small amounts as they are Rastafari holy colors
- Lining the eyes with eyeliner is not allowed as Rasta Empress
- Neither is plucking the eyebrows

I love to wear clear gloss, because it accentuates my lips and gives me a fresh feminine appearance with my Rasta Jewelry.

As a Rastafari Empress I wear just one makeup product on my face at a time, and I try to keep all my makeup natural looking.

Rasta Woman Financial Obligations to the faith

Charity

"If he is in need, don't put off giving to him. Don't refuse to help a beggar who is in distress. Don't turn your back on a poor person..."

– "**Rasta Bible: Rastafari Spiritual Wisdom**"

Rastafari believe in Charity. We understand that *Charity is an Expression of Jah*. As Rastafari women we have a financial obligation to give to the poor and to help the needy.

Perhaps you would feel most comfortable making a donation online, however as Rasta wc know Jah has elected us to do the work others do not want to. (Feeding the poor, caring for the needy) *in person.*

Rasta women are not ashamed or afraid to "give" to people begging for change or to who live on the streets and have others see us. We know Jah sees and knows all things, and that we are his ambassadors and his messengers.

I as an Empress make a charitable donation to the poor every time I get paid. That's twice sometimes 3 times a month.

I simply take $5 or $10 out of my purse and hand it to someone I believe to be homeless and living on the street, or I give the money to someone who is holding a cup outside a coffee shop (begging for change.) I as a Rasta Empress enjoy doing this because I know it is part of the financial obligation of my spirituality. Therefore when Jah sees me caring for his creations, I get blessings I never saw coming.

Do Rasta women help those who ask her for money?

Q: What should you do as a Rasta woman if someone *directly* asks you as an Empress to borrow some money or a beggar *directly* asks you to have some money when you are out in public and you have enough money in your purse to cover the amount they are asking for?

A: It is your Responsibility as a Rastafari Empress to help those in need. Those in need are not always homeless; sometimes they are just "in need." As Rasta we never *turn up our noses* to those in need we try to help them if we are asked, in private or in public.

#8 Rastafari Rules for women who are Single

- Single Rasta women are not allowed to sleep with men who are not Rasta
- Single Rasta women are patient and pray to Jah to send a Rastafari King man at the right time

- Single Rasta women do not masturbate
- Single Rasta women do not look at or read pornography
- Single Rasta women do not visit non Rastafari night clubs
- Rastafari women are <u>not allowed</u> to have sex with Bald Heads!

Single Rastafari women are encouraged to

- Mingle with other Rastafari online
- Meet other Rasta at Rastafari events
- Make friendships with others who study the Holy Christian bible
- Single Rastafari women *are allowed* to date Christian men because Christianity is a part of Rastafari. He does not have to convert to Rastafari for you to be his Empress.

Are Rastafari women allowed to use Condoms?

One day I met a guy who told me he had sex with a Rasta Empress and she preferred to do it "Ital." This is a load of crap.

Rastafari women are allowed to use condoms; however we do not believe it healthy to take birth control such as "The pill." Most Kingman allow Empress to make the decision on her own to use birth control or to not use birth control.

#9 Rasta woman Rules for (Hair) dreadlocks Crown

- Every Empress must wear her hair in Dreadlocks or she is disrespecting the faith
  - Empress are not allowed to let non Rasta touch her dreadlocks
  - Empress must have hair covered in public at all times. This includes places of work, shopping malls, grocery stores etc.

- Empress is not allowed to cut, trim, comb, curl or braid the holy dreadlocks crown
- Empress must clean the dreadlocks by washing the dreadlocks at least 1 time per week with lime and aloe or natural shampoo
- Empress may dye dreadlocks to natural color to hide /cover grey. However most Rasta prefers to allow dreadlocks grey to show as this is a natural process of life.
- Empress may not use dreadlocks to attract sexual attention
- Empress does not have to have perfectly rolled roots as this hides the kink of the African coils, something Rasta are proud of. Even if your hair type is not African Rasta are not obsessive about dreadlocks roots being neat and tight.

- Empress hair may be worn down and loose when Empress is with her King man
- Empress holy dreadlocks crown is a symbol of Jah to always be respected, kept clean and maintained as woman of the Rastafari Livity.

Other hair on Empress Body

No hair on the body of Empress is to be trimmed cut or waxed or plucked. It is to grow freely for all the days of an Empress life. This is a symbol of our covenant with, and dedication to Jah.

I haven't shaved my arm pit hair or the hair on my legs or in "other parts." In 6 years. I feel free, and less vain. I spend less money too. Any man that is truly Rasta will be turned on by Rasta woman's "natural" appearance.

Give thanks to Jah for putting me on the right road, and directing me away from Babylon "lye" and Vanity!

#10 5 Reasons Rastafari Women Cover Their Locks in Public

1. A true Rasta woman covers her hair to show spiritual respect to the Most High and other deep Rasta, she may encounter.

2. A true Rastafari woman covers her locks to maintain a *private* spiritual

relationship with only the creator, while in public!

3. A true Rasta woman covers her dreadlocks while in public to reserve some of her beauty only for her Rasta King and her family and herself.
4. A true Rasta woman wraps her hair in an upward spiral to provide more of a Queen appearance (as they do in parts Africa)
5. A true Rasta woman covers her hair to keep private that part of her that is sacramental.

#11 6 things to Google about Rastafari

It is the duty of Every Rasta do to their own Research. Nobody can do it for you. Part of the fun is the discovery. Here are some thing you can Google and read books about to get you up to speed.

- "King Dawit"
- "King Selassie I"
- "King Menelik"
- "Queen of Sheba and King Solomon"
- "Marcus Garvey"
- "Bob Marley Interviews on YouTube"
- "A.J. Rodgers books"
- "How Europe underdeveloped Africa"
- "Suzar the meaning of dreadlocks"

#12 Rasta Women Rules for Holidays

Holidays not celebrated by Rasta Empress

- Christmas
- Easter
- Thanks Giving
- New Year's Day
- Valentine's Day

We as Rasta say that these holidays have meaning that is Babylonian, it's just that most people don't know. Google it or ask a Rastafari.

Rastafari Holidays celebrated by Empress

- Jamaica Independence Day– **August 06 2016**
- King Selassie I birthday – **July 23**
- King Selassie I Coronation day – **November 2nd**
- The day King Selassie I Visited to Jamaica – **April 21st (Groundation Day)**
- Marcus Garvey Birthday – **August 17**

#13 Rasta women as Role Model in the community

- Rasta women do not walk the street late at night after dark
- A Rasta woman does not believe she is better or worse off than anybody else. Therefore we are friendly with all people, rich poor, young old etc.
- Rastafari women offer to lend a helping hand whenever the

opportunity arises because we know Jah Jah is watching

- Rasta women speak good things about others or not at all
- Rasta women do favors for people and don't ask for money or anything else in return.
- Rasta women watch her friend's children any time it is needed.

#14 9 Things Rasta women are forbidden to do!

- Drink Alcohol
- Smoke Cigarettes
- Wear pants in public
- Swear in public
- Take Pharmaceuticals
- Take Street Drugs
- Cut or Trim Dreadlocks
- Eat Meat or pork
- Hang out in the street
- Gossip about others

#15 10 Things Every Rastafari woman must have in her home

1. **Pictures and or Art that celebrate African Beauty** – Rastafari is a celebration of African Roots and Culture. We embrace and love to look at African Beauty.
2. **Books on Natural Medicine –** Rastafari love to treat their bodies with *Natural* Medicine, Instead of

Babylon Pharmaceuticals. We do not believe in the use of Pharmaceuticals. We as Rasta believe pharmaceuticals make people sick in the long run

3. **Books about the Life of Marcus Garvey, King Selassie I, Bob Marley** - There are 3 Main leader of the Rastafari Movement. King Selassie I, Marcus Garvey, King Selassie I. Rasta love to read about the history and lives of these leaders.

4. **Incense Burners** - For the Sabbath (Nag champ, Frankincense etc.) and or just to change up the vibes in the home.

5. **Lion of Judah Flag** – The Lion of Judah flag is the International symbol of the Rastafari Movement. Rasta can feel the spirit of King Selassie I and Empress Menen emanate from this flag.

6. **King Selassie I photo / Plaque Photo -**
7. **Rastafari Reggae Music**; Capleton, Sizzla, Dennis Brown, Bob Marley, Garnett Silk, I Wayne etc.
8. DVDs on African American History
9. **Natural cleaning products –** Empress love to assist the environment with staying healthy. We believe in natural cleaning products for the earth.
10. **King James Version Bible –** This is the main reference book for Rastafari spiritual guidance and Heritage.

#16 Nyahbinghi Guidelines for Rasta Women

The Nyahbinghi woman must abide by Emperor Haile Selassie I Ivine laws. During I-semble, the Nyahbinghi women are responsible for the teaching of the children with special emphasis on the Amharic languages, His Imperial Majesty Emperor Haile Selassie I, Black History and other aspects of Rastafari Ivine livety.

She is not permitted to administrate around the altar or to prophecy before the congregation. A Nyahbinghi queen does not play the drums at an I-semble but does play the SHAKA (Shaker) or TIMBREL. She may participate in governmental administration, as in the taking of minutes, writing/reading of letters or any other works she is capable of doing, as seen by the House. She should also strive to improve her livity and skills/education so that she may be of greater strength to the Theocracy of Emperor Haile Selassie I and the family.

She must be attired in modest apparel at all times and must not wear pants or revealing garments. Her head must be covered during an I-semble or when congregating among the brethren or outside her gates.

As H.I.M. is the Head of the Nyahbinghi Order, the Nyahbinghi queen must recognise her Kingman as her head. She must be loyal to her king head in all things concerning righteousness and at all times. If there is a misunderstanding between her and her king man, the matter should be brought before the priest or the Council of Elders who will deal with the matter privately and constructively. During her monthly issue (period of 7 days), the Nyahbinghi queen does not attend, I-semble or congregate among the brethren's.

When the Nyahbinghi queen brings forth a prince, she should stay away from an I-semble for a period of 3 months. If she brings forth a princess, she should stay away for a period of 4 months.

The Nyahbinghi woman must abstain from whoredom, adultery, fornication and all sinful acts that are an abomination to the Most High. She should keep her temple clean, refraining from use of flesh, drugs, alcohol and all harmful articles of food that are forbidden. The wearing of jewelry is not forbidden but the piercing of the ears is against the will of JAH. The plaiting of locks is forbidden as it is written in the book of II Peter 3: 3, "Whose adorning let it not be that outward adorning of plaiting the hair." The Nyahbinghi woman is nonviolent, non-abusive and non- partisan. She must also be free from all corruption as a true daughter of JAH Rastafari.

#17 Rules for Rasta Women who are married

- Rastafari women do not aim to have an orgasm during sexual Intercourse. We have sex with our Kingman to express love.
- Rastafari women do not discuss relationship or sexual issues outside of the relationship
- Rasta women do not have intercourse during her menses

In case you were wondering...

Kingman may have another Empress if Empress agrees otherwise it is not allowed. The reason is King Selassie I had only ONE Empress. That is Empress Menen. To have multiple Empresses is disrespect to the Faith. *True* Rasta men know this.

Rastafari women do not have to be legally married to be married under Rastafari. Living together constitutes a marriage under Rastafari

Rastafari Women Responsibilities to Kingman

1. To be a trusted friend
2. To provide encouragement in the Relationship
3. To encourage Kingman to reach higher and move up in life and always do better for himself and the family
4. To keep the home clean
5. To serve hot fresh nutritious Ital meals at meal times
6. To ensure that clothing and washing of clothes and other household duties are taken care of providcd Kingman is working outside of the home and is the sole income provider for the family

7. To provide love and affection to Kingman on a regular consistent basis
8. To be a strong spiritual support.
9. To be Monogamous and keep her body clean at all times
10. To respect his desires and wishes for all concerning the family and household.
11. To serve King in a manner that is respectful and loving at all times.

I serve my Kingman, and I am happy to do it. It's not something I do because my faith calls for it. It's something I do to honour Jah. Honouring Jah with or without a Rasta man is my life. My King serves me too. We have an unspoken rule. Don't make the Empress/Kingman have to ask you twice.

I love it.

#18 7 Principles of Rastafari

Rastafari Principle #1: "Rasta does not eat meat"

Meat is dead flesh. As instructed by the Most High, to keep the temple clean, the eating of dead flesh is strictly forbidden.

The meat was alive but is now dead. All dead animals have a spirit. Only Jah knows where the spirit of dead animals lingers.

Not eating meat, allows for us to feel ourselves as being more light weight.

By eating a diet that is strictly fruits and vegetables as its base, combined with other spiritual practices, we are able to more experience ourselves as our soul.

Rastafari Principle #2: "Keep the temple Clean"

It is easy for one to defile his temple with unclean sex acts etc.

Promiscuity

Masturbation

Group Sex

Prostitution etc.

Rasta does not ingest...

Medication (Babylon tricks, to make you sicker)

Alcohol (avoid the devils drink)

Cigarettes

Recreational drugs

Rasta use herbs for his ailments, and smoke the natural plant of The Most High- Marijuana, for pleasure and meditation.

How to keep the temple clean as Rasta

Practice Monogamy when with a mate

Practice celibacy when without a mate

Stay away from all "unclean" sexual acts, thoughts, and images

Eat food that is "non processed" and in its original form

We as Rasta know that to keep the temple clean, is one of the most important assurances for entrance into holy Mount Zion (heaven)

Temple cleanse as Rasta

Many Rasta like to do a "cleanse" of the body about once a month, to release toxins. Visit your local health food store to purchase an all-natural herbal cleanse kit.

Rastafari Principle #3: "Rasta does not cut the hair"

Rasta does not cut, shave, trim or pluck any hair, anywhere on the body. This is in keeping with the covenant that Rasta has written by The Most High on his heart.

Rasta Covenant with Jah

The growing of the dreadlocks is the physical representation of the Rasta Covenant with Jah, the Almighty...

The Rastafari covenant is as follows...

"Jah, I am yours....I will no longer cut trim or alter any hair on my body in honour of you.

I understand that once I begin to grow my locks, this covenant must never be broken, otherwise I have committed a Sin against the most high.

I vow to honour you all the days of my life in all things that I do.

I vow to be clean in words and deeds, and to do all I can to include you in my daily living.

I vow to keep your 10 commandments.

Please bless and guide me, oh Jah protect me. I am yours from this day forward. My promise is to serve you, all the days of my life."

Two major points have been covered by this covenant...

I will keep your 10 commandments oh Jah

I will honour you all the days of my life.

This is why Rasta allows the hair on the legs, chest, eyebrows, armpits, and face, to grow, and grow, without, shave trim or cut...all the day of our lives!

Rastafari Principle #4: "Freedom of Self"

Freedom of Self is one of the most important Rastafari principles for living. Rasta believes all Men and Women of all Nations should be free. Rasta believes that to have a job is a form of slavery. Therefore in Babylon, many people are not free.

Self-Employment

Rasta strongly believes in self-employment, for the purpose of self-freedom, creative freedom, and freedom of spiritual practices. As Rasta we like to pray, meditate, and read bible verses, whenever we are in the mood to do so.

Jah should take precedence in places of employment

Creativity, Individuality, and leadership is the natural road to prosperity

Instead many people have forgotten about The Almighty, and have become "out of touch" with their own creativity and Individuality which further gives into the "slave" mentality of Babylon.

Rastafari Principle #5: "Honour Jah"

Jah is a black African Spirit! All born Rasta, from all parts of the world, know this. This is what makes us Rasta!

How to Honour Jah

By wearing the hair in dreadlocks

By mounting a photo of King Selassie I in the Home

By wearing (Rasta) Ethiopian (African) colors Red Yellow and Green

By learning about black history - the history of all people

Rastafari Principle #6: "Resist Satan"

Another very important part of embracing the Rastafari livity is to "Resist the Temptations of Satan" Rasta knows the temptations of Satan are many.

Satan knows our hearts

Satan knows our minds

Satan knows our weaknesses

Here is a list of just some of the temptations of Satan

Stealing

Lying

Promiscuity

Self-hatred

Sexual perversion

Committing a crime

Abusing others

Suicide

Prostitution

As Rasta we "Reject" all thoughts and actions related to Satan. We try to avoid all places, people, and things, which are governed by Satan.

Satan Comes in Many Forms

It could be...

The urge to do something "wild"

An Invitation to go to a certain "cool" place

The desire to make some "quick cash"

The feeling to take "revenge" on an enemy

The desire to "impress" a woman or man, girl or boy

Rastafari Principle #7: "Unity"

In

Rastafari Unity means 2 things: Unity by and for the black nation and world unity for all Nations

Rasta Love and Respect the African Nation

Black slavery has caused the Unity and culture of black people to crumble. For this reason, as appointed by Jah, all Rasta whether he is black, whether he is white, whether he is Indian, whether he is Asian, etc. He must have love for and respect for, the black African nation.

#19 6 Rules to live Natural as Rasta Woman

Natural Living is "Zion living." This includes *the food you eat, how you care for your Body, and how you care for and maintain your home.*

#1 Do not Drink Cow's Milk

Empress and Kingman drink Almond Milk or Soya Milk Only! <u>Rasta does not believe in drinking Cow's milk.</u> It is nonsensical, and deemed *"unclean."*
Many Rastafari shop at health food Grocery stores, or bulk food stores because we can meet most of our *Ital* food needs by shopping this way.

#2 Clean home with Natural cleaning products

No Aerosol Spray cans (we know aerosol spray contains harmful chemicals to the environment. (CFCs)

"Thursday Plantation" Tea tree Oil

Rasta uses all natural cleaners for cleaning the home and doing chores such as dishes and laundry around the house. I use "Tea tree Oil." It's great for cleaning anything in the home including, floors and dishes. It Smells great and it's all natural Just dilute it in some water before using it.

Look for the "Thursday plantation" brand. (Yeah I am not thrilled about the name either) But it really is one of the better brands for "Tea Tree" Oil products.

#3 heal the body naturally

For Health and Healing Rastafari do not believe in taking prescription medications. *We use vitamins, minerals and herbs.*

I own a great book for this purpose...it's called...

"The Doctors Complete Guide to Vitamins and Minerals" (Buy it on Amazon.com)

From this book I have learned that there is a vitamin or a mineral you can take for just about anything that ails you. Prescription drugs are not a necessity. This is a Great book to Guide you to live without the use of Medications as A Rastafari Empress!!!

#4 Use natural body soap

All natural, without additives or preservatives. Here in Toronto, Canada, we have store called *"Lush."* You can find them online as well. They make all natural soaps and hair care products that smell *out of this world*. My favorite soap is called "Karma."

#5 Use natural toothpaste;

Rasta is aware that there are some potentially harmful ingredients in toothpaste. The most common knowledge of the harm regular Toothpaste can do to the body is that it can assist in the calcification of the "Pineal Gland," which is one of, our spiritual gateways, locate in the center of the brain between the eyebrows and is responsible for our psychic (sixth sense) connections.
The ingredients on toothpaste are just too long. Rasta use all natural "Neem" toothpaste, or "Tea Tree" toothpaste to brush our teeth. Or you can use plain old baking soda.

#6 Wash Dreadlocks with Natural Shampoo

Many people don't give a second thought to the type of shampoo they wash their hair with. As Rastafari Empress we pay special attention to this. Remember our hair is our "spiritual Antenna." It is very important that we honour Jah and use Shampoo that is natural, and not harmful to our bodies as our hair is a "sender and receiver" of spiritual energy and information, our hair follicles are a super absorbent part of the body.

Many Jamaican Rasta use a mixture of Aloe and lime to wash the Dreadlocks. It is said to help the hair to lock. This is true if you go out immediately into the sun after you wash your hair with the mixture.

#20 "Empress to Empress" Code of Conduct

There is a certain gentleness every Rastafari woman carries. She takes her responsibilities and her role and duties as Rastafari to heart. She may be silent should she become disappointed but when it comes to another Empress she gives her all. Two Empress sharing one space must get a long, and maintain a positive free flowing energy relationship for Jah.

Empress to Other Empress do not....

- Empress never tells another Empress how to embrace Rastafari
- Empress never gives advice regarding an Empress Kingman
- Empress do not Gossip about the life of another Empress

Empress to Other Empress Always...

- Empress to Empress show the Highest amount of Respect for one another as fellow Royalty
- Empress always show love and Encouragement and Sisterhood to

other Empress, treating her as she would her own sister

- Empress do not hold onto old Grudges with other Empress. We let them go and understand that <u>each day is a new.</u>

In Rastafari we have a *natural Brotherhood and Sisterhood.* Always showing love and Respect to one another. We are not a part of Babylon so we always demonstrate that we are *higher* than Babylon by our words actions and deeds particularly towards another Rasta.

#21 6 Ways Rasta women Submit to their Rasta King

A woman should only "submit to" her Rasta King if it is "written on her heart" to do so. Born Rasta women do this willingly and naturally, here I give you some tips on how to make it happen naturally, and the thought processes I keep submitting to my Rasta King.

#1 Know when to keep silent

Know when to just "shut up!" I know this is going to be hard for women who have been taught to *"fight for your rights" and to "express yourself", and "don't let any man talk down to you"* blah, blah blah, but when it comes to a relationship of Rastafari, both the King and Queen have to *practice silence.* It is wise to know when you should just, keep silent.

Staying silent doesn't mean anything other than, staying silent. It is the quality of a true Rasta woman to know when to be the beautiful feminine energy and just use your silence to make your point. Many people don't know what to do in the middle of an argument, when all of a sudden the other person goes silent. Try it and see for yourself.

#2 Let him win

Your Rasta King is the head of the relationship. Remember he is also full of testosterone. Sometimes it is best to just let him win. It makes a Rasta King feel good to know his Empress trust his word and that he knows what he is talking about or knows what he is doing - even when you, as Empress, may know better. Let your Rasta King win most of the time, this is what a true Rasta woman does. Ok? Ok.

#3 Be Gentle

Be gentle with your Rasta king. Rasta men have extra sensitive hearts. You may not know it but your Rasta King may be feeling many things that you as his Rasta Empress, do and say, very deeply. Be gentle, with your tone, don't belittle him, and try to use nice words when expressing frustration. Utilizing just these tools alone will go a long way to keeping the harmony between you and your Rasta King smooth and argument free.

#4 don't make him ask you twice

If you want to behave as a true Rasta Empress, You must know Rule #1. <u>Don't make your Rasta King Ask your twice</u>. If he makes a request, get on it right away, or answer him immediately as to why you cannot attend to it right away and tell him when you will. Me as a Jamaican Rasta woman, these are the things I would do. These suggestions are not to make women subservient, I am simply sharing with you what is written on my heart as far as my love for my Rasta King. This takes us to the next point.

#5 never argues with him in public

A Rasta Empress never argues with her Rasta King in public. Save your feelings and thoughts for when you are in private. A Rasta Empress must exercise self-control. To lack self-control, is to lack the presence and holiness of Jah. Rasta Empress must always behave "Queenly" when in Public, arguing in public with anyone is not allowed!

#6 be the first one to give in

Try to be the first one to give in during or after a disagreement. The bible says *"those who exalt themselves will be humbled, and those who humble themselves will be exalted."* To give in during a disagreement means allowing the force and love of Jah to take precedence over the desire of the ego to "win" and be right. The next time you have a disagreement with anyone, including your Rasta King, try to be the first one to give in. Ladies if your Rasta man is physically abusive to you, or talks down to you, it's not because he is a Rasta; it is because he is an idiot. Real Rasta men don't put their hands on women in an aggressive manner. The acceptance of physical abuse is not a part of the Rastafari way of life, or Rastafari love relationships.

Before you submit, Make sure he is a true Rasta man...

Make sure your Rasta King is a True Rasta man before you submit. A true Rasta man will appreciate you doing these things. So, the question is, how can you tell if your man is a real Rasta?

Is he patient, and understanding?

Does he love children?

Does he say such and such is a "blessing"?

Does he refer to Jah at least 1 time per day?

Does he read his bible "religiously"? Does he spend long periods of time alone?

Was he a Rasta when you met him?

Does he abstain from drinking alcohol and smoking cigarettes, and eating meat?

Does he say nice things about Jamaica and or his birth country?

Does he just look at you sometimes and you don't know what he's thinking?

Does he compliment you a lot.....?

Does he accept "no" when you tell him you don't want to have sex?

Does he verbal his appreciation for African beauty?

I don't believe in submitting to a man who is not a true Rasta or who doesn't respect and appreciate me as much as I appreciate him.

I once was asked by an Empress who was living with a King and had children, if it was ok under the Rastafari Livity to have many Empress. It is not ok actually. Very simply for the component of cleanliness. Sharing your genital with more than one person can cause sickness or even death. Born Rasta do not participate in such a lifestyle. Don't allow men who are not Rastafari to fill your head with excuses of why *he can or cannot* do certain things. Investigate. Visit my blog and ask me.

#22 Natural Ital Food Rules & Recipes

Ital Food Rules for Rasta

Learning to cook and eat like a Rasta may be a lot simpler than you think. We have 5 rules for maximum spiritual and physical well-being type cooking.

- o Without additives and or preservatives
- o No Meat and no Pork ever!
- o No Salt (Sea Salt is acceptable in small amounts while cooking)
- o Some Rasta do not eat chicken (they feel it is the same as eating red meat)
- o Some Rasta do not eat eggs or fish (this is a personal choice)
- o *I personally eat chicken about once every 30 days for the protein.*

An Ital (vegan) Rasta diet is best! As long as you follow these simple rules, you are cooking an Ital Rasta meal.

How to Cook steamed Jamaican Cabbage

1 medium cabbage

2 tablespoon margarine

1 scotch bonnet pepper (cut up and add for spicy)

2 sprig thyme

1 crushed garlic or 2 teaspoons garlic powder

2 or 3 small slices of a sweet green pepper.

1 medium chopped onion or 2 tablespoon onion powder

Black pepper

Salt to taste

1/4 cup water

Preparation

Wash cabbage

Cut up/slice cabbage leaves in pieces.

Sauté onion, garlic, pepper, thyme in margarine.

Add cut up cabbage water and stir.

Cover saucepan and cook cabbage are tender.

Add whole scotch bonnet pepper

Sprinkle with pepper and salt.

Simmer then serve with avocado pear.

How to cook Spicy Eggplant

INGREDIENTS:

2 medium-size eggplants (about 2 lbs), peeled and cut into 3/4" pieces

1 tbsp. oil

5 garlic cloves, minced

2 tsp minced fresh ginger

1/2 cup chicken bouillon, or vegetable broth

2 tbsp. soy sauce

2 tbsp. rice vinegar

1 tsp. dark sesame oil

1 tbsp. sugar

1 tsp. hot chili-garlic sauce

4 scallion, chopped

1 or 2 tomatoes, coarsely chopped

Preparation

Heat oil in a large non-stick pan or wok.

Stir fry eggplant until slightly darkened, from 2 to 3 minutes.

Reduce heat, and add garlic, ginger and stir-fry for 1 minute.

Add bouillon, soy sauce, vinegar, sesame oil, sugar and chili-garlic sauce and bring to boil.

Cook, uncovered and stirring often, until eggplants are tender and sauce has thickened, about 5 minutes.

Stir in onions and tomatoes, and season with salt to taste.

Cook 5 more minutes. Sprinkle with sesame seeds if you wish.

How to cook Rasta Ital Soup

You will need....

1 Pound (454) g Yams or about 2 medium sized Yams cut into 2 inch 5 cm pieces

½ pound (227 g) sweet potatoes (1 medium, cut into 2 inch (5 cm) pieces

1 can of coconut milk

3 cups (720 ml) vegetable broth

1 pound (454) fresh pumpkin or butternut squash, peeled and cut into 2 inch (5 cm pieces

½ pound (227 g) carrots (3 medium) peeled and sliced

1 Pound (454g) Fresh callaloo, or 1 can (19 ounces (538 g) callaloo, drained; or ½ pound of spinach and ½ pound (227g)

Kale
1 Chayote squash
1 Green pepper
2 medium sized tomatoes
2 cloves garlic
3 spring onions or scallions
5 - 6 cups shredded cabbage
1 hot pepper, minced
Freshly ground black pepper and salt

How to Prepare
Step 1
Place the yams and sweet potatoes in a stockpot with the coconut milk and broth. Add the pumpkin or squash and carrots.

Step 2
Bring to a boil and simmer for 10 minutes.

Step 3
While the root vegetables simmer, carefully wash the callaloo, trimming away any thick stems. Chop and set asides

Step 4
To peel the chayote squash, cut it lengthwise into quarters and remove the heart. Dice the remaining squash, green

pepper, tomatoes, garlic, and spring onions, and add with the shredded cabbage and hot pepper to the stockpot.

Step 5
Simmer for 20 minutes more until the vegetables are tender. Season with plenty of freshly ground black pepper and salt if desired. Puree the vegetables for richer soup. Makes 6 servings

How to cook Jamaican "Run Down"

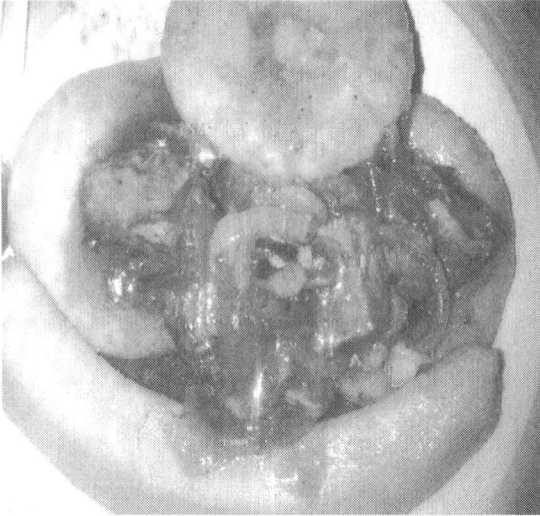

If you want to embrace the Culture of Jamaica, then you have to eat some "Run Down" at list once on a Sunday Morning with some Fried dumpling. Seriously it hits the spot and may send you back to bed, that's what it does to me. One Jamaican man I knew, called "Run Down" "slave food." My opinion is that it tastes great and is great to make on a budget, and is easy to cook.

Don't worry about the name; it won't give

you a runny stomach. The name comes from the rich gravy of the meal.

You will need...

3 tablespoons of freshly squeezed lime juice

2 lbs. (1 kg) mackerel or other oily fish (salt fish *boneless* works good too)

3 cups (750) coconut milk

1 large onion, diced

2 cloves garlic, sliced

1 scotch bonnet or jalapeno chili, deseeded and minced

1 lb. (500 g) ripe tomatoes, blanched, peeled and diced

1 tablespoon cider vinegar

1 teaspoon dried thyme

Salt and freshly ground black pepper (no salt if you are using salt fish)

How to Prepare
Step 1
Pour the lime juice over the fish fillets in a shallow bowl and set aside.

Step 2
IN a large, heavy skillet cook the coconut milk until it turns oily about 5 to 7 minutes.

Step 3
Add the onion, garlic and chili, and cook until tender, about 5 minutes
Stir in the tomatoes, vinegar, thyme, and salt and pepper.

Step 4
Add the fish, cover and cook until the fish flakes easily when tested with a fork, about 10 minutes.

How to cook Jamaican Curried Tofu

1 pound of tofu
Light soy sauce
Little bit of sea salt and freshly ground black pepper
½ teaspoon ground cumin
½ teaspoon garlic powder
½ Teaspoon of Jamaican curry powder
2-3 tablespoons of olive oil
1 medium onion diced
1 medium potato, peeled and cut into cubes
3 / 4 cups of baby carrots
1 medium roma tomato diced
2 scallions chopped

5 sprigs of fresh thyme
½ teaspoon of ground allspice
1 cup of water
1 vegetarian bouillon cube
15 ml of flour
Dissolved in 45 ml of water

Step 1

Drain the Tofu and slice it into 8 - 10 pieces.
Sprinkle both sides lightly with the soy sauce, and season to taste with the salt, black pepper, cumin, garlic powder, and curry powder

Step 2

Heat the oil in a large skillet over medium high heat and add the tofu, and fry on both sides until firm and golden.
Transfer it to a plate and set it aside

Step 3

Add more oil to the skillet if needed, then add the onion, potato, and carrots and sauté until tender.

Step 4

Season with a pinch of salt and add the

tomato, scallions, thyme, allspice, 1 cup of water and bouillon

Step 5

Bring to a boil, then add the flour and water mixture and cook until the sauce begins to thicken

Step6

Return the tofu to the skillet and simmer for approximately 10 minutes.
serve over rice or vegetables
Makes 6 Servings

Please go to amazon.com and give

"Life as a Rasta Woman" a Rating.

Blessed Love.

www.jamaicanrastafarianlove.com

Rastafari Beliefs & Principles

Jah Rastafari Prayers

JAH RASTAFARI
PRAYERS

Empress Yuajah

Rasta Way of Life

How to Become a Rasta

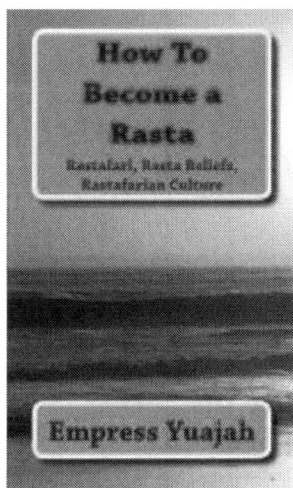

Rastafari For African Americans

RASTAFARI

AFRICAN AMERICAN
SPIRITUALITY

EMPRESS

Rasta Meditation Handbook

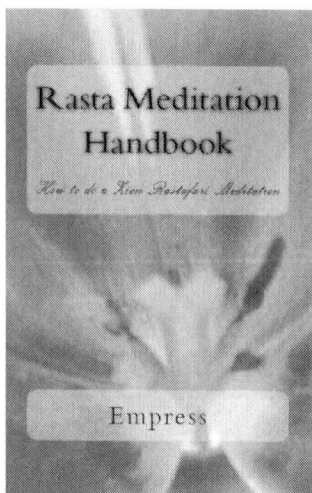

About the Author

Empress thought she was *done* writing books on Rastafari Culture, until one day she decided to "deepen" her faith. Not too long after this decision, she felt *called* to write *"Rasta Bible: Rastafari Book of Wisdom."* And *"Life as a Rasta Woman."* She is also the Author of *"Rasta Way of Life"* and *"Rastafari: Beliefs and Principles"* available on amazon.com
www.jamaicanrastafarianlove.com

17599708R00062

Printed in Great Britain
by Amazon